NATIONAL GEOGRAPHIC KiDS

WORLD ATLAS
STICKER ACTIVITY BOOK

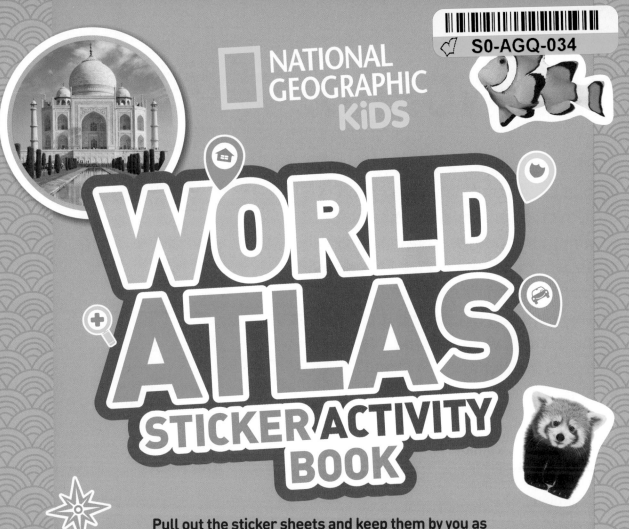

Pull out the sticker sheets and keep them by you as you complete each page. There are extra stickers to use in this book or anywhere you want! Have fun!

NATIONAL GEOGRAPHIC
Washington, D.C.

Consultant: Martha Sharma
Designed by Callie Broaddus and Sanjida Rashid
Editor: Priyanka Lamichhane; Photo editor: Lori Epstein
Cartographer: Mike McNey

PICTURE CREDITS: AL = Alamy Stock Photo; DS = Dreamstime; GI = Getty Images; IS = iStockphoto; NGP = National Geographic Partners; SS = Shutterstock

1 (UP LE), Byelikova Oksana/SS; 1 (UP RT), Kletr/SS; 1 (CTR RT), Eric Isselee/DS; 1 (LO LE), Viktor Gmyria/DS; 1 (LO RT), nattanan726/SS; 2 (UP), Eric Isselee/DS; 2 (LO LE), Ariel Skelley/Blend Images LLC/GI; 2 (LO RT), Eric Isselee/SS; 3 (UP LE), Wim Wyloeck/DS; 3 (UP CTR), Andrey Podkorytov/AL; 3 (UP RT), Aureliy/SS; 3 (CTR), Anan Kaewkhammul/SS; 3 (LO LE), JG Swanepoel/IS; 3 (LO RT), Eric Isselee/DS; 4 (LE), Tom Middleton/SS; 4 (RT), Michel Piccaya/SS; 5, Sekar Balasubramanian/IS; 6 (fruit market), Curioso/SS; 6 (pizza), bestv/SS; 6 (Mexico City), Diego Grandi/SS; 6 (jade masks), David Coventry/National Geographic Image Collection; 6 (small seashells), Photodisc; 6 (conch shell), Irina Rogova/SS; 6 (cockleshell), Denis Tabler/SS; 7 (LE), Michael Coffman/SS; 7 (RT), Dan Breckwoldt/SS; 8 (UP LE, UP RT), FloridaStock/SS; 8 (LO), Eric Isselee/SS; 9 (UP), James Pintar/SS; 9 (CTR), Steven Oehlenschlager/DS; 9 (LO LE), Emi/SS; 9 (LO RT), Chriswood44/DS; 10 (UP LE), Ana Vasileva/SS; 10 (UP RT), Nataliya Hora/SS; 10 (LO), Eric Isselee/SS; 11 (sugar), givaga/SS; 11 (bananas), Maks Narodenko/SS; 11 (chocolate), M. Unal Ozmen/SS; 11 (soccer ball), DS; 11 (LO RT), Sabena Jane Blackbird/AL; 12 (alpacas), Eric Isselee/SS; 12 (Easter Island statue), Viktor Gmyria/DS; 13 (UP), Eric Isselee/SS; 13 (CTR), Pyty/SS; 13 (LO), Calavision/SS; 14 (Amazon River), Johnny Lye/SS; 14 (red-eyed tree frog), Sascha Burkard/SS; 14 (blue morpho butterfly), digitalimagination/IS; 14 (poison dart frog, facing left), kikkerdirk/IS; 15 (poison dart frogs), Dirk Ercken/DS; 15 (caiman), Eric Isselee/SS; 15 (macaws), Mayskyphoto/SS; 15 (piranha), DS; 15 (howler monkey), Octavio Campos Salles/AL; 16 (UP), Ramon Carretero/SS; 16 (LO), Cedric Weber/SS; 17 (UP LE, LO), Charlotte Dirkse/SS; 17 (UP RT), Ostranitsa Stanislav/SS; 18 (LE), Viacheslav Lopati/SS; 18 (RT), Photodisc; 19 (windmill), JeniFoto/SS; 19 (toy sailboat), Jules Kitano/SS; 19 (cloud), sumroeng chinnapa/SS; 20 (LE), Jim Nelson/SS; 20 (RT), Suranyi Mate/SS; 21 (UP), leoks/SS; 21 (CTR), dschreiber29/IS/GI; 21 (LO), Wrangel/DS; 22 (lioness & cub), Maggy Meyer/SS; 22 (blue butterfly), Bildagentur Zoonar GmbH/SS; 22 (Samburu women), hecke61/SS; 22 (yellow butterfly), pan demin/SS; 22 (orange butterfly), Andre Coetzer/SS; 23 (UP), oneo/SS; 23 (LO LE), Dietmar Temps/SS; 23 (LO RT), Nebojsa Markovic/SS; 24 (UP LE), alexsvirid/SS; 24 (UP RT), sculpies/SS; 24 (LO), EQRoy/AL; 24 (baboon), Samantha Reinders/SS; 25 (UP LE), Adisa/SS; 25 (UP RT), AlexeiLogvinovich/SS; 25 (LO LE), Tom Grundy/AL; 25 (LO RT), AlexAranda/SS; 26 (UP LE), Andrzej Kubik/SS; 26 (UP RT), Andy Dean Photography/SS; 26 (LO), johan63/IS; 27 (giraffes), pandapaw/SS; 27 (lioness), GlobalP/GI; 27 (zebra), vblinov/SS; 27 (baby elephant), Andre Klopper/SS; 27 (baby zebra), Johan Swanepoel/SS; 27 (elephant), Talvi/SS; 27 (lion cub), Eric Isselee/SS; 27 (termite mound), Simon Greig/SS; 27 (eagle), wildpix/SS; 28 (UP), Eric Isselee/SS; 28 (LO LE), Eric Isselee/DS; 28 (LO RT), Katvic/SS; 29 (UP), zummolo/SS; 29 (LO LE), Anna Kompanieitseva/SS; 29 (LO RT), Eric Isselee/SS; 30 (UP LE), Maks Narodenko/SS; 30 (UP RT), Samart Mektippachai/SS; 30 (LO), Eric Isselee/DS; 31 (UP), vvoe/SS; 31 (LO), Byelikova Oksana/SS; 32 (hiker), Olga Danylenko/SS; 32 (lake), Natalia Davidovich/SS; 32 (Mount Everest), Daniel Prudek/SS; 32 (rope), BonD80/SS; 32 (helmet), Normana Karia/SS; 32 (boots), Marek CECH/SS; 33 (snow leopard), Stayer/SS; 33 (Tibetan village), Jef Wodniack/SS; 33 (Sherpa), RichardBaker/AL; 33 (Tibetan fox), Wang LiQiang/SS; 33 (red panda), Eric Isselee/DS; 33 (finch), Eric Isselee/SS; 33 (peacock), Alfredo Falcone/DS; 34 (LE), Eric Isselee/SS; 34 (RT), Uwe Aranas/SS; 35 (UP), PicturePartners/IS; 35 (LO), GlobalP/IS/GI; 36 (oystercatcher birds), David Steele/SS; 36 (cable car), Milosz Maslanka/SS; 36 (triton shell), Fotana/SS; 36 (scallop shell), Alexander Raths/SS; 36 (round seashell), Nyvlt-art/SS; 36 (sea star), Peteri/SS; 37 (Māori people), Anders Ryman/Corbis Documentary/GI; 37 (sheep), Inna Astakhova/SS; 37 (border collie), Eric Isselee/SS; 37 (Sydney Opera House), Selfiy/SS; 37 (toy boat), Photodisc; 37 (airplane), Nerthuz/SS; 37 (rubber duck), Sergiy Kubyk/SS; 38 (UP), Ian Scott/SS; 38 (LO), R. Gino Santa Mar/SS; 39 (clownfish), Kletr/SS; 39 (Great Barrier Reef), Tanya Puntti/SS; 39 (dugong), Andrea Izzotti/SS; 40 (LE), Vladimir Seliverstov/SS; 40 (RT), Wildlife GmbH/AL

Printed in Malaysia
21/IVM/4

THE WORLD

Earth is made up of seven large pieces of land called continents surrounded by large water bodies called oceans. Each continent has people, animals, and places that make it special. This drawing of Earth's continents is called a map. On this map, north is at the top, south is at the bottom, west is to the left, and east is to the right.

Each continent has animals that are found only there. Sticker the animals near the continent where they're found.

BUFFALO

CULTURE SNAPSHOT

Our world is made up of seven continents and is home to more than seven billion people.

NORTH AMERICA

ATLANTIC OCEAN

PACIFIC OCEAN

SOUTH AMERICA

ALPACA

* SPACE DOES NOT ALLOW THE LABELING OF ALL 195 COUNTRIES. TO SEE ALL OF THE COUNTRIES LABELED, REFER TO MAPS IN THE *NATIONAL GEOGRAPHIC KIDS BEGINNER'S WORLD ATLAS.*

** POPULATION IS THE SUM OF CONTINENTAL POPULATION AS SHOWN IN THIS ATLAS, BASED ON 2017 DATA.

CHAMOIS

Europe and Asia are one landmass divided by the Ural Mountains.

Every continent is made up of landforms, such as mountains and rolling plains.

ARCTIC OCEAN

EUROPE

ASIA

TIGER

AFRICA

PACIFIC OCEAN

INDIAN OCEAN

AUSTRALIA

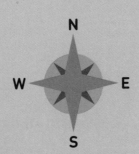

N

W   E

S

GIRAFFE

ANTARCTICA

KANGAROO

NORTH AMERICA

North America is shaped like a triangle. It is wide, cold, and frozen in the north. In the south, it is very narrow, hot, and steamy. Canada, the United States, and Mexico make up most of the land of North America, but there are lots of other countries in Central America and the islands of the Caribbean.

How many countries are in Central America?

....

Arctic Region

Alaska (part of the United States)

PACIFIC OCEAN

San Francisco •

Los Angeles •

Orcas live in oceans worldwide. They can be spotted off the **WEST COAST OF THE U.S.A. AND CANADA.** A group of orcas is called a **POD.**

GEOGRAPHY SNAPSHOT

The **COUNTRY OF PANAMA** is a narrow strip of land at the southern part of North America. The Panama Canal was dug through this strip of land to allow large ships to sail directly between the Atlantic and Pacific Oceans.

ARCTIC OCEAN

FLAG OF THE U.S.A.

Use the locator pins to mark the places you want to visit in North America.

Greenland (part of Denmark)

The **BALD EAGLE** is the national **SYMBOL OF THE UNITED STATES.**

A r c t i c   R e g i o n

MAP KEY
★ Capital city
● Other city

CANADA

FLAG OF CANADA

Ottawa ★

Chicago ●

● New York

Washington, D.C. ★

Canada is the **LARGEST COUNTRY IN NORTH AMERICA,** and the second largest country in the world. Canada has two official languages: English and French.

UNITED STATES

ATLANTIC OCEAN

CUBA

HAITI

DOMINICAN REPUBLIC

MEXICO

Mexico City ★

Santo Domingo ★

C a r i b b e a n

BELIZE

HONDURAS

JAMAICA

GUATEMALA

Central America

Guatemala City ★

Panama Canal

PANAMA

EL SALVADOR

★ Panama City

NICARAGUA

COSTA RICA

5

PEOPLE AND PLACES

Every place on Earth has its own culture—made up of language, food, clothing, customs and celebrations, music, and art. Most people in North America live in towns or cities. The two languages most often spoken are English and Spanish. People enjoy foods from all over the world.

Circle the four differences between the pictures.

CULTURE SNAPSHOT

MEXICO CITY, MEXICO, is home to more than 21 million people. It is the largest city in North America.

How many shells can you find? ....

People in Costa Rica shop for **FRUITS AND VEGETABLES** at the local **MERCADO,** or market.

Find the missing Maya mask and circle the one that is different.

HISTORY SNAPSHOT

The *LINCOLN MEMORIAL* in Washington, D.C., U.S.A., honors Abraham Lincoln, the 16th president of the United States.

Sticker the missing parts of the totem pole.

Draw a totem pole that tells a story about your family. Are there colors, symbols, or patterns that remind you of your family traditions?

Along the **WESTERN COAST** of Canada and the United States, native people carve **TOTEM POLES** to tell stories about their **FAMILIES** and **CULTURE.**

THE FAR NORTH

The Arctic Ocean borders North America in the far north. The land and much of the ocean are covered part of the year with snow and ice. Animals such as polar bears, arctic foxes, reindeer, and snowy owls have adapted to the extreme cold. Walruses have layers of fat that enable them to live in the cold waters of the Arctic Ocean.

The **NORTH POLE** is in the frozen Arctic Ocean.

Help the mommy polar bear find her cub.

WILDLIFE SNAPSHOT

REINDEER, called caribou in North America, move in herds from place to place in the cold far north in search of food.

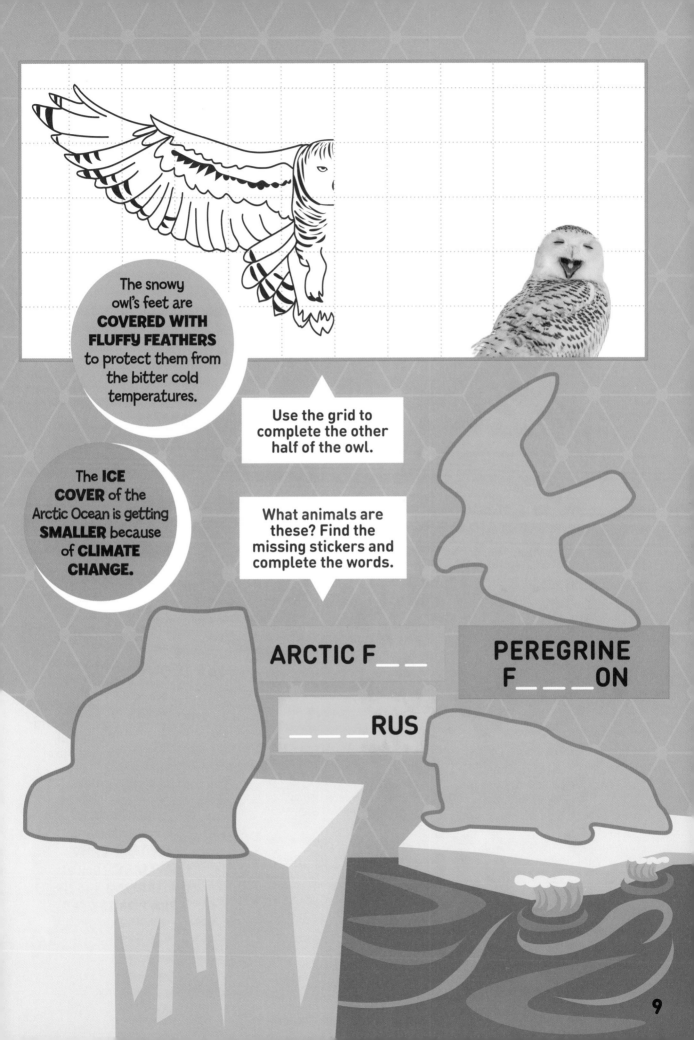

The snowy owl's feet are **COVERED WITH FLUFFY FEATHERS** to protect them from the bitter cold temperatures.

The **ICE COVER** of the Arctic Ocean is getting **SMALLER** because of **CLIMATE CHANGE.**

Use the grid to complete the other half of the owl.

What animals are these? Find the missing stickers and complete the words.

ARCTIC F_ _ _

PEREGRINE F_ _ _ _ON

_ _ _ _RUS

SOUTH AMERICA

South America is home to the world's driest hot desert, the Atacama, and its largest rainforest, the Amazon. The Amazon River in Brazil carries more water than any other river in the world. The Andes Mountains extend all the way from Colombia in the north to Chile and Argentina in the south.

FLAG OF CHILE

Galápagos Islands
(part of Ecuador)

GEOGRAPHY SNAPSHOT

The **ATACAMA DESERT** is located mainly in northern Chile. A place near the center of this desert has never recorded any rainfall.

Easter Island
(Rapa Nui)
(part of Chile)

South America is home to many **ENDANGERED ANIMALS,** such as the **JAGUAR** and the **GIANT ANTEATER.**

Sticker the places you want to visit in South America.

Bananas, chocolate, coffee, and sugar are all **FOODS PRODUCED IN COLOMBIA.**

GUYANA

SURINAME

VENEZUELA

French Guiana (part of France)

Bogotá ★

ECUADOR

COLOMBIA

Andes Mountains

Amazon River

Amazon

PERU

Machu Picchu

Lima ★

BRAZIL

BOLIVIA

Atacama Desert

ATLANTIC OCEAN

PARAGUAY

São Paulo •

Rio de Janeiro •

Andes Mountains

SOCCER is the most **POPULAR SPORT** in South America.

ARGENTINA

Santiago ★

Buenos Aires ★

CHILE

MAP KEY
★ Capital city
• Other city
■ Point of interest

URUGUAY

PACIFIC OCEAN

CULTURE SNAPSHOT

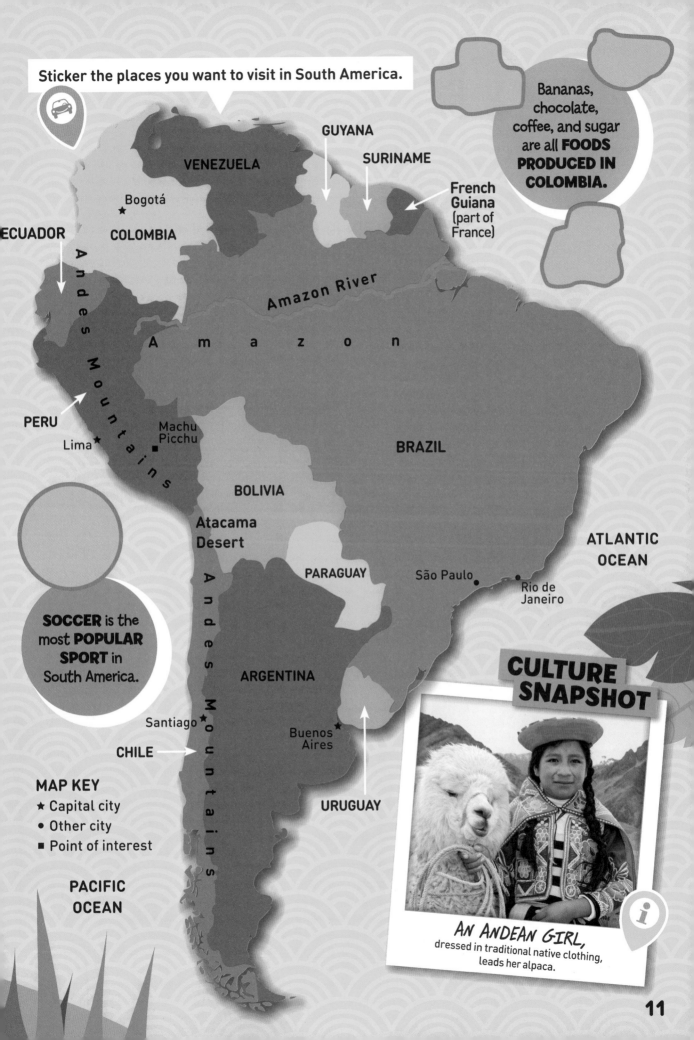

AN ANDEAN GIRL, dressed in traditional native clothing, leads her alpaca.

PEOPLE AND PLACES

South America has a rich cultural heritage. Native people, including the Inca, were the first to settle in the region. They were followed by Europeans and Africans. Each group brought customs and traditions that make up the culture of South America today. Most people speak either Spanish or Portuguese. But in the mountains, native languages are still spoken.

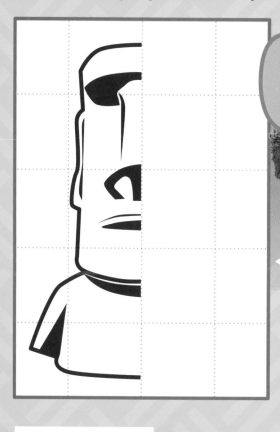

Use the grid to complete the other half of the statue.

Sticker sweaters on the alpacas.

Easter Island is a part of Chile. Located in the Pacific Ocean, the island is home to **HUNDREDS OF GIANT STATUES** that were carved from rock by islanders more than **500 YEARS AGO.**

CARNIVAL is a celebration in Brazil, South America's largest country. It marks the **BEGINNING OF LENT,** a time of religious observance that comes before Easter. It includes colorful parades and masks and lively dancing and music.

Color the Carnival mask.

FLAG OF PERU

ALPACAS are native to Peru. Their **SOFT AND SILKY FLEECE** is used to make woven items such as **SWEATERS.**

HISTORY SNAPSHOT

Ruins of the Inca city of *MACHU PICCHU* in Peru are almost 600 years old.

Connect the dots to complete the drawing of the guitar, then color it in.

1
2
3
4
5
6
7
8
9
10
11
12
13
14
15
16
17

The **GUITAR** was brought to South America **BY SPANISH SETTLERS** in the early 1600s and is a very popular musical instrument there today.

13

AMAZON RAINFOREST

The Amazon rainforest is the largest tropical rainforest in the world. Most of the Amazon rainforest is in Brazil, but it extends into eight countries in South America. It is home to more kinds of plants and animals than any other place on Earth.

There are **MORE THAN 2,000 TYPES OF BUTTER-FLIES** in the Amazon rainforest.

GEOGRAPHY SNAPSHOT

The **AMAZON RIVER** is 4,345 miles (6,993 km) long.

MORE THAN 1,000 SMALLER RIVERS enter the Amazon River as it flows from its source in the Andes Mountains to the Atlantic Ocean.

Sticker the frogs and butterflies.

Color the flying macaw.

WILDLIFE SNAPSHOT

BLACK HOWLER MONKEYS
are louder than any other type of monkey. Their howls can be heard from more than three miles (5 km) away.

How many frogs can you find? ....

More than **1,000 TYPES OF FROGS ARE FOUND** in the Amazon rain-forest.

Help the caiman find its dinner.

CAIMAN

PIRANHA

EUROPE

Europe is the second smallest continent, but it has many countries. Russia, the world's largest country, is in both Europe and Asia, but it is counted in Europe because its capital city, Moscow, and most of its people live in the European part of Russia. People in Europe have farmed and raised animals for many years, but today most people live in towns and cities.

FAST FACTS

➔ **NUMBER OF COUNTRIES:**
46 (INCLUDING RUSSIA)

➔ **POPULATION:**
751,632,000

FLAG OF RUSSIA

ICELAND

The **IBERIAN LYNX** lives in Spain and Portugal. It is the **MOST ENDANGERED MEMBER** of the cat family.

IRELAND

NETHERLAND

UNITED KINGDOM

Stonehenge ■ ★ London

BELGIUM

Paris ★

ATLANTIC OCEAN

FRANCE

PORTUGAL

Madrid ★

SWITZERLAND

SPAIN

Mediterranean Sea

HISTORY SNAPSHOT

STONEHENGE
is a ring of standing stones in the southern United Kingdom. It is almost 5,000 years old.

GEOGRAPHY SNAPSHOT

Sticker the places you want to visit in Europe.

FJORDS IN NORWAY
are deep, narrow valleys cut by glaciers and flooded by the sea.

ST. BASIL'S CATHEDRAL, built in 1561, is no longer a church, but it is an important landmark in Moscow, the capital of Russia and the largest city in Europe.

SWEDEN

FINLAND

RUSSIA

NORWAY

MAP KEY
★ Capital city
● Other city
■ Point of interest

DENMARK

LATVIA

LITHUANIA

★ Moscow

GERMANY

POLAND

BELARUS

CZECHIA

AUSTRIA

UKRAINE

HUNGARY

Milan

ITALY

ROMANIA

SERBIA

Vatican City

BULGARIA

TURKEY

Istanbul ●

GREECE

★ Athens

BRAN CASTLE, located in the Transylvania region of Romania, is, according to legend, the residence of **COUNT DRACULA.**

Mediterranean Sea

PEOPLE AND PLACES

The 46 countries of Europe vary in size from tiny Vatican City to Ukraine, the largest country entirely within Europe. These countries represent the many different culture groups that make up the continent. Most groups have their own language and customs. Many of the cities and towns in Europe are very old.

Located in Paris, France, the **EIFFEL TOWER** stands at 1,063 feet (324 m) and has **20,000 LIGHT BULBS** that make it shine bright at night.

Sticker toppings on the pizza.

HISTORY SNAPSHOT

The **PARTHENON** in Athens, Greece, was built nearly 2,500 years ago as a temple dedicated to the Greek goddess Athena.

The history of **PIZZA** can be **TRACED TO ANCIENT TIMES,** when toppings were added to flat breads.

Circle the four differences between the pictures.

FLAG OF THE
NETHERLANDS

WINDMILLS
are an important piece
of the history of the
NETHERLANDS.
Most were used to
DRAIN WATER from
swampy land.

Find the country names and sticker their flags.

FRANCE

GREECE

ITALY

LATVIA

SWEDEN

F	E	I	I	Y	E	L	L
I	R	K	W	C	L	A	E
L	K	A	E	H	N	T	N
A	Y	E	N	E	Y	V	F
F	R	W	D	C	D	I	X
G	Q	E	K	L	E	A	S
M	W	H	I	T	A	L	Y
S	N	G	J	C	X	A	N

MEDITERRANEAN SEA

The Mediterranean is a large sea, almost completely surrounded by Europe, Africa, and Asia. Its water is deep blue. The land around the Mediterranean has hot, dry summers and cool, rainy winters. Many plants and animals live in and around the sea. It is also a popular vacation destination.

WILDLIFE SNAPSHOT

BARBARY APES
are the only wild monkeys found in Europe. They can be seen sitting on walls high above the Spanish coastline.

OSPREYS
live along the Mediterranean coast or near rivers, where **THEY CATCH FISH,** the main food in their diet.

Connect the dots to complete the drawing of the devil ray.

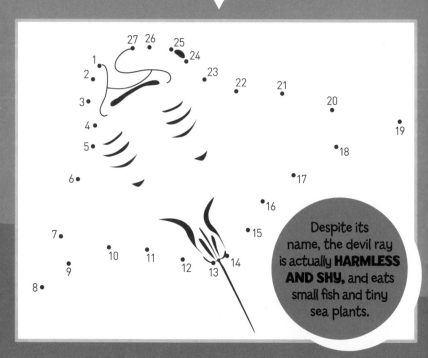

Despite its name, the devil ray is actually **HARMLESS AND SHY,** and eats small fish and tiny sea plants.

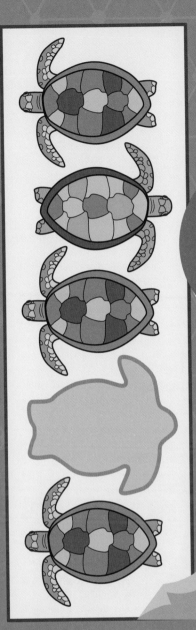

Find the right sticker to complete the pattern of loggerhead sea turtles.

LOGGERHEAD TURTLES are the **MOST COMMONLY FOUND** turtles in the Mediterranean Sea. Loggerheads eat clams, crabs, and even jellyfish.

GEOGRAPHY SNAPSHOT

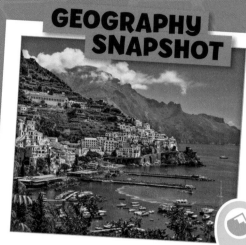

A town sits on the rocky Amalfi Coast of the **MEDITERRANEAN** above fishing boats at anchor in southern Italy.

Help the monk seal find its food.

MONK SEALS live mainly in the waters of the eastern Mediterranean.

OCTOPUS

AFRICA

Africa is a continent of deserts, tropical rain-forests, and tall grass savannas. People travel from around the world to visit Africa's wildlife parks. Most people in Africa live in rural villages, but there are also busy modern cities, such as Lagos, Nigeria, and Cairo, Egypt.

FAST FACTS

➲ **NUMBER OF COUNTRIES:**
54

➲ **POPULATION:**
1,215,763,000

Marrakesh

Western Sahara (part of Morocco)

MAURITANIA

GUINEA

ATLANTIC OCEAN

CÔTE D'IVOIRE

CULTURE SNAPSHOT

MAASAI WOMEN
of East Africa are known for their colorful beadwork. Each color has special meaning—for example, white for peace, blue for water, red for bravery.

Sticker butterflies into the grass.

Lions **LIVE IN GROUPS** called **PRIDES.** Tourists often visit Africa for wildlife safaris in order to see lions and other large animals, such as **ELEPHANTS, ZEBRAS,** and **GIRAFFES.**

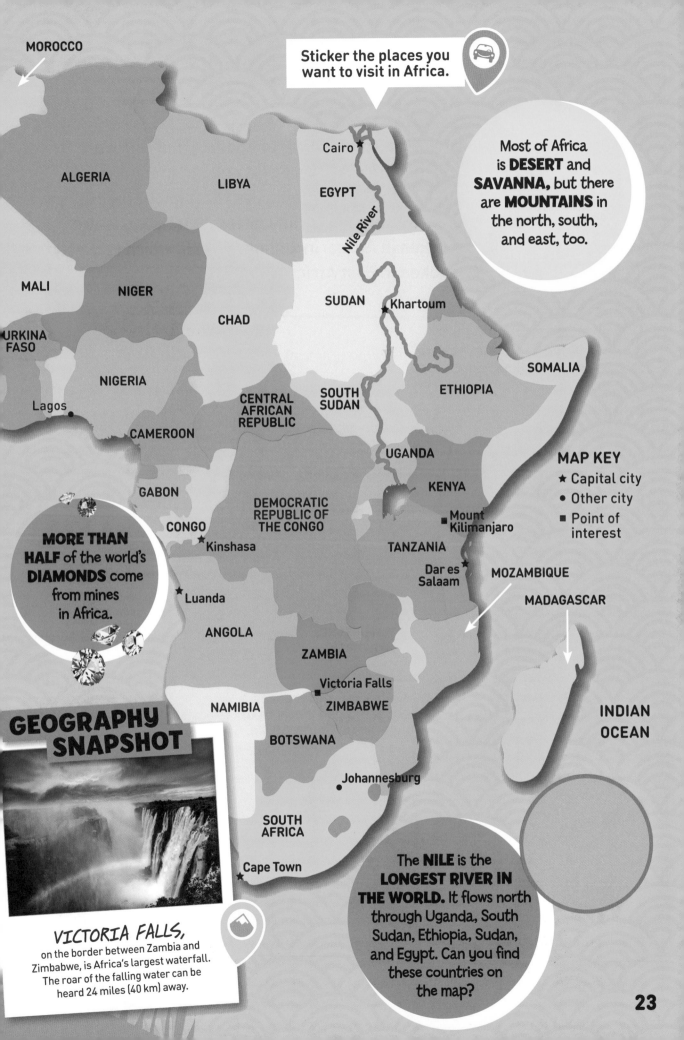

MOROCCO

Sticker the places you want to visit in Africa.

Cairo ★

ALGERIA

LIBYA

EGYPT

Nile River

Most of Africa is **DESERT** and **SAVANNA**, but there are **MOUNTAINS** in the north, south, and east, too.

MALI

NIGER

CHAD

SUDAN

Khartoum ★

URKINA FASO

NIGERIA

CENTRAL AFRICAN REPUBLIC

SOUTH SUDAN

ETHIOPIA

SOMALIA

Lagos ●

CAMEROON

UGANDA

MAP KEY
★ Capital city
● Other city
■ Point of interest

GABON

DEMOCRATIC REPUBLIC OF THE CONGO

KENYA

MORE THAN HALF of the world's **DIAMONDS** come from mines in Africa.

CONGO

Kinshasa ★

■ Mount Kilimanjaro

TANZANIA

Dar es ★ Salaam

MOZAMBIQUE

★ Luanda

MADAGASCAR

ANGOLA

ZAMBIA

INDIAN OCEAN

Victoria Falls ■

NAMIBIA

ZIMBABWE

GEOGRAPHY SNAPSHOT

BOTSWANA

Johannesburg ●

SOUTH AFRICA

The **NILE** is the **LONGEST RIVER IN THE WORLD.** It flows north through Uganda, South Sudan, Ethiopia, Sudan, and Egypt. Can you find these countries on the map?

Cape Town ★

VICTORIA FALLS, on the border between Zambia and Zimbabwe, is Africa's largest waterfall. The roar of the falling water can be heard 24 miles (40 km) away.

PEOPLE AND PLACES

Africa has many different people and cultures. Arab cultures are in Egypt and other countries in the north. Tribal people live throughout the rest of Africa. More than 1,500 different languages are spoken in Africa, including Swahili, which is widely spoken in East Africa.

MASKS are important in African culture. They have special meanings related to **RELIGION, CUSTOMS,** or **CEREMONIES.** Most masks are patterned after either a human face or an animal head.

Design your own mask.

HISTORY SNAPSHOT

The **GREAT PYRAMIDS** in Egypt are more than 4,000 years old. They were built as tombs during a time when Egypt was a powerful civilization led by kings called pharaohs.

Circle four differences between these pictures of Cape Town, South Africa.

Colorful houses line the streets of the **BO-KAAP** neighborhood in **CAPE TOWN,** South Africa. The name Bo-Kaap means "above the cape."

CULTURE SNAPSHOT

AFRICAN SPICE MARKETS, such as this one in Marrakesh, Morocco, are filled with many colors and smells. People use spices, peppers, and herbs to flavor their food.

Find the names of the spices.

BASIL	GARLIC
CAYENNE	GINGER
CINNAMON	VANILLA

C	G	A	R	L	I	C	C
F	I	H	G	U	E	A	A
G	M	N	T	G	L	C	Y
X	I	C	N	L	Q	L	E
A	I	N	I	A	I	N	N
N	D	N	G	S	M	A	N
V	A	W	A	E	O	O	E
V	F	B	T	R	R	Q	N

Color in a traditional South African Zulu basket.

Zulu baskets are **HANDMADE** in South Africa using natural plant materials such as **GRASSES** and **LEAVES.** Different patterns have special meanings.

THE SAVANNA

The African savanna is a tropical grassland with trees and shrubs. The climate is warm year-round. The savanna is home to many animals, including elephants and giraffes. Meat-eating animals, such as lions, cheetahs, and hyenas, hunt large herds of grazing animals, such as zebras and antelope. Birds, insects, and reptiles live here, too.

GEOGRAPHY SNAPSHOT

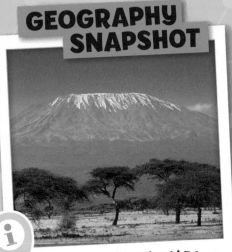

ⓘ **MOUNT KILIMANJARO** rises above the savanna grasslands in Tanzania. It is the highest mountain in Africa.

Find the right stickers to complete the pattern of rhinos.

RHINOS wallow in **MUD POOLS** to cool off and also to **PROTECT THEIR SENSITIVE HIDE** from the sun and from parasites.

LILAC-BREASTED ROLLERS perch on treetops, where they can spot insects and other small animals to eat. They swoop down to grab their prey.

Color in the drawing of the lilac-breasted roller by matching each color below to its corresponding number on the bird.

1 = ▬	4 = ▬
2 = ▬	5 = ▬
3 = ▬	6 = ▬

Sticker the missing animal babies and match them to their moms.

Zebras live in the wild only in Africa. A **ZEBRA'S STRIPES** are like fingerprints— no two zebras have the same stripe pattern.

GEOGRAPHY SNAPSHOT

A *TERMITE MOUND* in Botswana towers over a giraffe. The mound is a mixture of soil, termite saliva, and dung. Mounds are found throughout the savanna.

AFRICAN FISH EAGLES eat fish, but they also catch and eat waterbirds, such as flamingoes. They live near **RIVERS** and **FRESHWATER LAKES** throughout southern Africa.

Sticker the missing puzzle piece to see what the eagle caught.

ASIA

Asia is a land of extremes! It is the largest continent. It has the world's highest point (Mount Everest) and its lowest point (the Dead Sea). More people live in Asia than on all the other continents put together.

Asia is the only place where **TIGERS, GIANT PANDAS,** and **COBRAS** live in the wild.

FAST FACTS

→ **NUMBER OF COUNTRIES:** 46 (NOT COUNTING RUSSIA)

→ **POPULATION:** 4,402,007,000

Sticker the panda.

Istanbul
TURKEY
ISRAEL
Dead Sea
IRAQ
IRAN
SAUDI ARABIA
Rub' al Khālī
YEMEN   OMAN   Karachi

INDIAN OCEAN

GEOGRAPHY SNAPSHOT

LAKE BAIKAL
in Russia is the world's oldest and deepest freshwater lake. It is more than 5,000 feet (1,524 m) deep.

CULTURE SNAPSHOT

The **TEA CEREMONY** is an important part of Japanese culture.

RUSSIA

Lake Baikal

KAZAKHSTAN

UZBEKISTAN

MONGOLIA

JAPAN

Tokyo

Osaka

Beijing

Tianjin

AFGHANISTAN

PAKISTAN

CHINA

Shanghai

Lahore

H i m a l a y a

Delhi

Chongqing

NEPAL

Mount Everest

BHUTAN

Guangzhou

INDIA

Dhaka

Shenzhen

PACIFIC OCEAN

Kolkata

Mumbai

Manila

Bengaluru

MYANMAR

VIETNAM

THAILAND

PHILIPPINES

MALAYSIA

I N D O N E S I A

Jakarta

More people speak **MANDARIN,** China's official language, as their first language than any other **LANGUAGE** in the world.

MAP KEY
- ★ Capital city
- • Other city
- ■ Point of interest

The **KOMODO DRAGON,** native to Indonesia, is the largest lizard living today.

GEOGRAPHY SNAPSHOT

FLAG OF SAUDI ARABIA

The *RUB' AL KHĀLĪ* in Saudi Arabia is the largest sand desert in the world. The name means "the Empty Quarter."

PEOPLE AND PLACES

Asia stretches from Russia in the north to Indonesia in the south and from Turkey in the west to Japan in the east. People come from many different cultures, speak different languages, and practice different religions. Many places have unique building styles and different forms of art.

Sticker the missing piece on the Japanese castle.

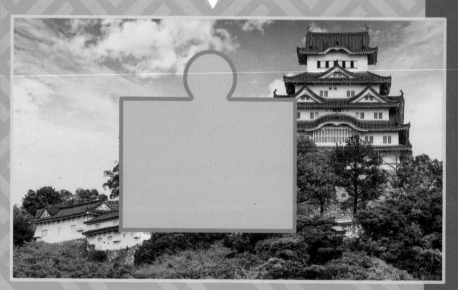

HIMEJI CASTLE IN KYOTO, JAPAN

Follow the lines to help the orangutan find its snack.

FLAG OF INDONESIA

ORANGUTANS live in the forests of Indonesia. They build nests high in the trees and live on a diet of **LEAVES, FLOWERS,** and more than 300 kinds of **FRUIT.**

CULTURE SNAPSHOT

CARPETS with vivid colors and designs are made by hand in Turkey, Iran, and other countries in western Asia.

CARPETS can be made of **WOOL, COTTON,** or **SILK.** Today, carpets may be made by machines, but the finest carpets are still made **BY HAND.** Carpets are usually named after the place where they were made.

Color in the carpet.

Sticker the missing pieces on the Taj Mahal.

The **TAJ MAHAL** was built in the 1600s and is a symbol of India's history and culture. **MILLIONS** of people visit it each year.

FLAG OF INDIA

THE HIMALAYA

The Himalaya stretch through Pakistan, India, Nepal, Bhutan, and China. This mountain range is home to some of the tallest mountains on Earth, including Mount Everest. But the Himalaya aren't just snowy peaks. There are forests and wetlands near the bottom of the mountains.

There are about 15,000 **GLACIERS** located throughout the Himalaya. There are also hundreds of **LAKES** in the region.

Help the trekker find the glacial lake.

FLAG OF NEPAL

Find the missing climbing gear.

Before **CLIMBERS** can begin their ascent of Mount Everest, they must move all of their **SUPPLIES** to a base camp at about 17,000 feet (5,000 m).

SNOW LEOPARDS live high in the mountains of Central Asia. Using their powerful hind legs, they can jump up to six times the length of their body.

Circle the four differences between these pictures of a Himalayan village in Nepal.

SHERPAS are members of a Himalayan ethnic group. They are known for their excellent mountain-climbing skills and often **HELP CLIMBERS** on their ascent of Mount Everest.

What animals are these? Find the missing stickers and complete the words.

RED PA _ _ _ _

PEAC _ _ _ _

TIBETAN F _ _ _

AUSTRALIA
AND NEW ZEALAND

Australia is the world's smallest continent and the only continent with just one country. East of Australia is the island country of New Zealand. There are also many other islands across the Pacific Ocean. Most people in Australia and New Zealand came from Europe originally, but there are also native people—Aboriginals in Australia and Māori in New Zealand.

INDIAN
OCEAN

A U S

O u t

Perth •

FLAG OF AUSTRALIA

AUSTRALIA has many animals, such as the **KOALA**, that are not found **IN THE WILD** anywhere else on **EARTH.**

Koalas live high in **EUCALYPTUS TREES.** They spend most of their time **SLEEPING**—up to 20 hours a day—or **EATING** eucalyptus leaves.

GEOGRAPHY SNAPSHOT

ULURU, also known as Ayers Rock, is a giant rock formation in the middle of Australia. It is sacred to the Aboriginals.

Sticker the places you want to visit in Australia and New Zealand.

KANGAROOS use their powerful hind legs to jump up to 15 feet (4.5 m) in a single hop. Female kangaroos, and also koalas, raise their babies in a pouch on their stomach.

Great Barrier Reef

T R A L I A

b a c k

■ Uluru

Brisbane •

NEW ZEALAND includes three main islands. North Island has active **VOLCANOES** and boiling **MUD POOLS,** while South Island has tall, snow-covered **MOUNTAINS.** Stewart Island is the smallest of the three.

Adelaide •

• Sydney

Melbourne •

FLAG OF
NEW ZEALAND

MAP KEY
★ Capital city
● Other city
■ Point of interest

PACIFIC OCEAN

Auckland •
North
Island

NEW ZEALAND

The **KIWI** is a **FLIGHTLESS BIRD** native to New Zealand, where it is the **NATIONAL BIRD.** Kiwis are about the size of a chicken.

South
Island   Wellington ★

• Christchurch

Stewart
Island

PEOPLE AND PLACES

Most people in Australia and New Zealand live in modern cities near the coast. Both countries were once British colonies, and English is the main language. In the middle of Australia, called the outback, there are large sheep farms and people live far apart from each other. Some children even attend school over the internet.

With almost 23,000 miles (37,000 km) of **COASTLINE,** Australia is known for great **SURFING.** Surfers come from around the world in search of the **PERFECT WAVE.**

GEOGRAPHY SNAPSHOT

In **WELLINGTON,** a cable car carries passengers up the hills that surround New Zealand's capital city. The city sits on the southern coast of North Island.

Draw and sticker your own design on the surfboard.

How many shore birds can you find?

Sticker shells onto the beach.

CULTURE SNAPSHOT

SHEEP were first brought to New Zealand in 1773 by British explorer Captain James Cook. Today, there are almost 30 million sheep in New Zealand.

The **MĀORI** were the original people of New Zealand. They settled in New Zealand more than 1,000 years ago. Today, Maori language, songs, and traditions are important parts of New Zealand's culture.

Rising above the harbor, the sails of the **SYDNEY OPERA HOUSE** are an **AUSTRALIAN LANDMARK** known around the world. More than one million people attend performances there each year.

Help the border collie find the sheep.

Start here

Circle the four differences between the pictures.

THE GREAT BARRIER REEF

Corals are tiny marine animals that live in warm coastal waters. Australia's Great Barrier Reef is the world's longest coral reef. It is made up of more than 3,000 individual reef systems and is home to more than 1,600 types of fish, as well as many other types of marine life, including sharks and turtles.

BLACKTIP REEF SHARKS are found in the warm waters of the Pacific and Indian Oceans, including the waters off northern Australia.

Sticker in the fins on the blacktip reef shark.

These **SHARKS** can be identified by the distinctive black coloring on the tips of their fins.

Color in the coral reef and sticker the fish.

WILDLIFE SNAPSHOT

BOX JELLYFISH are found in the coastal waters of northern Australia. They can have up to 60 tentacles, each with about 5,000 stinging cells. The venom in these cells is very poisonous. Watch out!

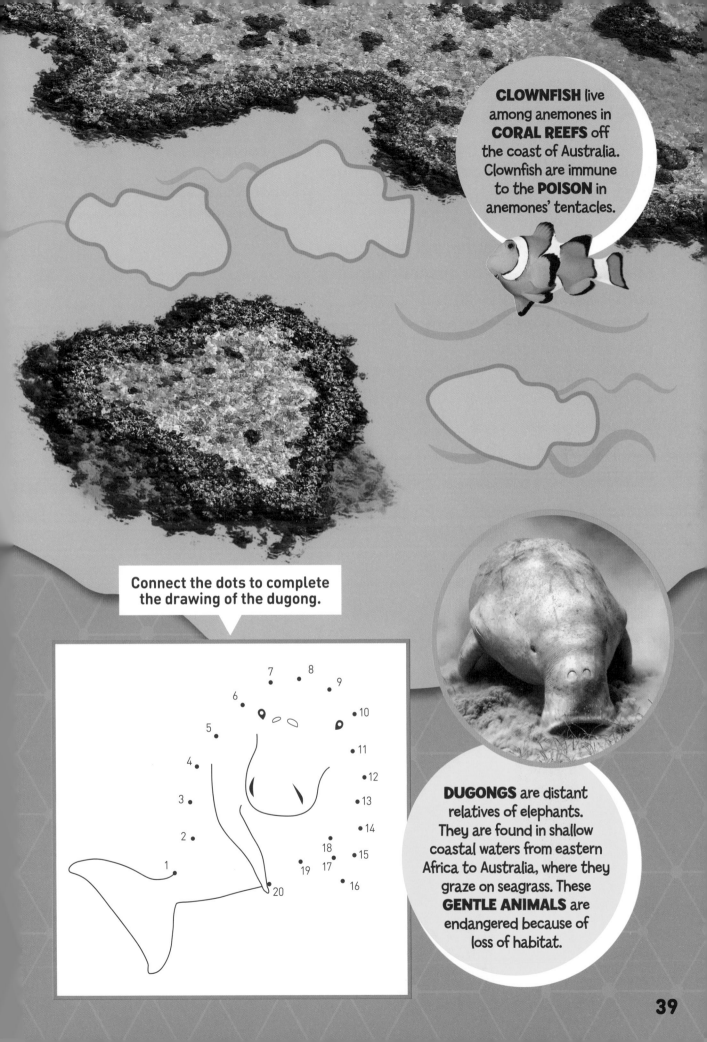

CLOWNFISH live among anemones in **CORAL REEFS** off the coast of Australia. Clownfish are immune to the **POISON** in anemones' tentacles.

Connect the dots to complete the drawing of the dugong.

DUGONGS are distant relatives of elephants. They are found in shallow coastal waters from eastern Africa to Australia, where they graze on seagrass. These **GENTLE ANIMALS** are endangered because of loss of habitat.

ANTARCTICA

Antarctica is the land around the South Pole. Most of Antarctica is covered by a layer of thick ice. No one lives in Antarctica permanently, but scientists spend time there to do research on climate and the environment. Some animals have adapted to the cold land and water conditions of Antarctica, including seals, penguins, and whales.

ATLANTIC OCEAN

INDIAN OCEAN

Antarctic Peninsula

ANTARCTICA

Ronne Ice Shelf

Amundsen-Scott Research Station

■ South Pole

MAP KEY
■ Point of interest

PACIFIC OCEAN

Ross Ice Shelf

McMurdo Research Station

Mount Erebus

Antarctica is home to many penguins. The **EMPEROR PENGUIN** is the largest penguin, weighing almost 90 pounds (40 kg).

Help the penguin find its dinner.

KRILL, tiny shrimp-like animals a little over two inches (6 cm) long, are an important **FOOD SOURCE** for animals in Antarctica.

pages 8–9

pages 10–11

Locator Pins

pages 12–13

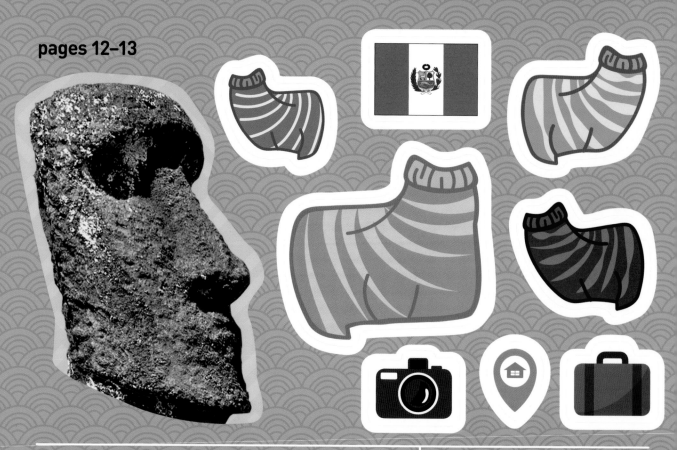

pages 14–15

pages 16–17

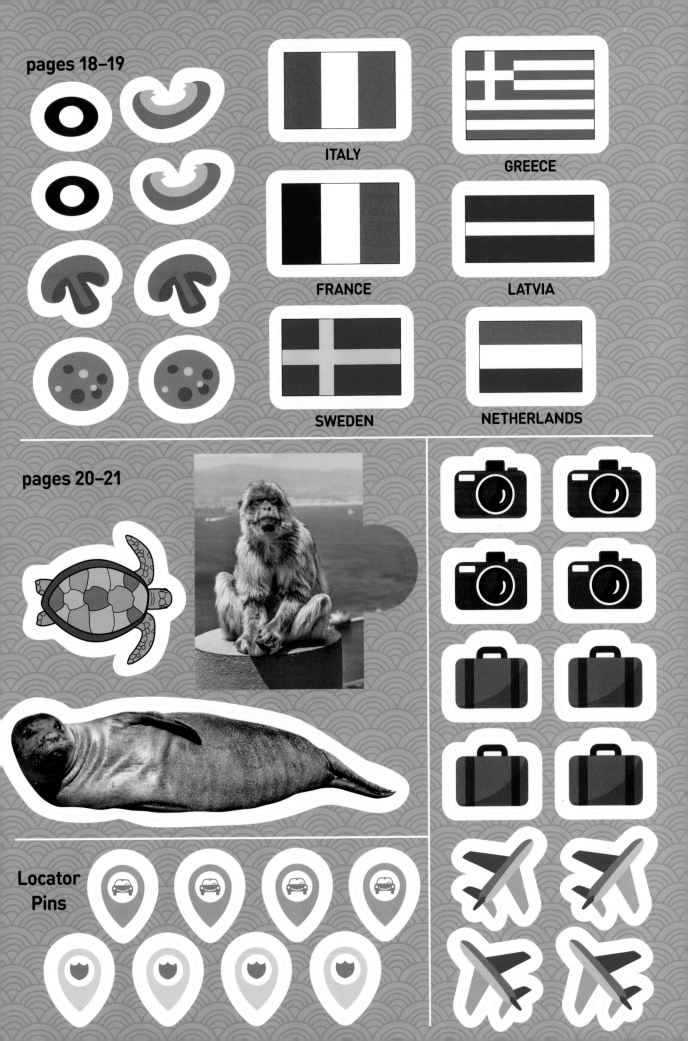

pages 18–19

ITALY

GREECE

FRANCE

LATVIA

SWEDEN

NETHERLANDS

pages 20–21

Locator
Pins

pages 22–23

pages 24–25

pages 26–27

Locator Pins

pages 28–29

SAUDI ARABIA

pages 30–31

Locator Pins

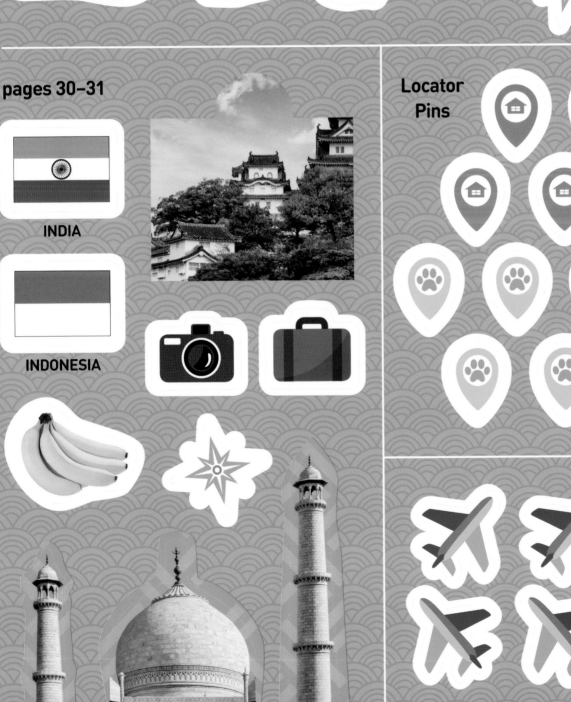

INDIA

INDONESIA

pages 32–33

NEPAL

pages 34–35

AUSTRALIA

NEW ZEALAND

Surfboard Designs

Locator Pins

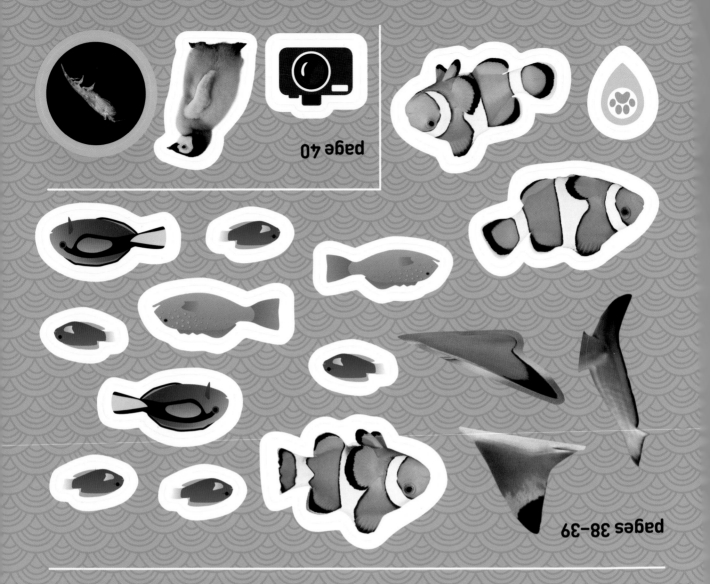

page 40

pages 38-39

pages 36-37